# DAUGHTER OF FAITH

# Daughter of Faith

## ALDIVAN TORRES

aldivan teixeira torres

# CONTENTS

# 1

# DAUGHTER OF FAITH

Daughter of Faith
Aldivan Torres

*Aldivan Torres is a writer consolidated in several genres. So far, the titles have been published in dozens of languages. From an early age, he was always a lover of the art of writing, having consolidated a professional career from the second half of 2013. He hopes, with his writings, to contribute to international culture, awakening the pleasure of reading in those who do not have the habit. Your mission is to win the hearts of each of your readers. In addition to literature, its main amusements are music, travel, friends, family, and the pleasure of life itself. "For literature, equality, fraternity, justice, dignity, and honor of the human being always" is its motto.*

## Daughter of Faith 1

## Kitchen

Mother
Good morning, my daughter. Sleep well?
Mary

Sort of, mom. The memory of Daddy remains disturbing me.

Mother

My God! How stupid you are. You still remember that damn thing that left us without any consideration. Take my advice and forget it forever.

Mary

I can't forget, mom. He was so affectionate to me. Please, do you know any news of him?

Mother

Yes. A letter arrived last week. He is living in São Paulo. He is reportedly working and living with another woman. Furthermore, he also sent money to help with his expenses, but I did not accept. I want nothing from that man. I just want away from him.

Mary

I understand your point of view, my mother. Thanks for the information. I also ask you to respect my feeling of daughter. Separation was really necessary. You didn't understand each other anymore and lived a daily hell. When love ends, there is nothing we can do.

Mother

I will respect your decision. I don't know if I'll ever forget all this. It is still very recent.

Mary

For sure, you will get over it. Time heals everything. I was also hurt by my father. But after six months of separation, there is a mixture of longing and anxiety.

Mother

This is normal. You are his daughter. However, I ask that we forget a little of the past. Let's live in the present and build our story. We need to live and survive.

Mary

We will do that. Let's go to the plantation?

Mother

Yes, let's go. It's time.

Trail-path

Daughter

Mom, what should I do to become a good woman?

Mother

You are already a good woman. Maintain the values of honesty, integrity and good repute. We are what we believe.

Daughter

It's ok. I'll do it. But how can I improve my life? Country life is so hard.

Mother

Work and study. There is no choice for the poor. What is your dream?

Daughter

I'm not sure yet. I just want to graduate as soon as possible and work on something.

Mother

I understand. I will support you all the time. I believe in your potential.

Daughter

I also believe in my talent. But things are so hard.

Mother.

What do you mean? Could you explain better?

Daughter

In addition to financial difficulties, I'm criticized by my colleagues for being a woman and black.

Mother

My God! What a terrible thing. But don't give up, daughter. Ignore these beings of darkness. Study hard and don't mind criticism. You are a powerful and talented woman. You are my pride.

Daughter

Thank you for supporting me. I will follow all your advice. I know I'm on the right track.

Mother

Believe it. For your contagious optimism, I will name you, "Daughter of the faith."

Daughter

It's a beautiful name. I will honor that name wherever I am. I will win!

Mother

So be it, my daughter!

Farm

Mother

Are you tired, daughter? We can stop if you want.

Daughter

Yes, I'm exhausted. Mom, I was here thinking. It's been a long time at work as a farmer. It is a noble work but exhausting. Does one day this panorama change?

Mother

It just depends on your efforts, daughter. I still want to see her leading her social class. I know you will not forget the poor.

Daughter

Truth. I will never forget my essence and my origins. I'm from these backwoods of my God. A place forgotten by elites and politicians.

Mother

I'm very proud of you. You are the angel that God sent to my house. Before that, my life was empty. You are our hope. I want to realize my dreams through you. There were so many dreams that I left behind.

Daughter

What were your dreams, mom?

Mother

I dreamed of being a dancer and an actress. But that was a big nonsense in my childhood. We lived in a situation of human misery and were forbidden even to study. These were times of suffering and darkness. I grew up determined not to repeat the same story with my children. A person's dreams are sacred. They are the ones who move us in everyday toil. This feeling of faith and hope is what keeps us alive. I am proud of my dreams even though I have not had a chance to make them come true. I will always support people pursuing their goals.

Daughter

It is truly a pity, my mother. Before you, I make a promise here: If I become a great woman, I will help you to fulfill your dreams. Dreams never die. While there is life, there is hope.

Mother

I thank you. But don't worry about me. Stay focused on your goals that God will bless you. Trust the almighty. He knows all the things.

Daughter

I have complete confidence in God and in myself. I don't know when it will happen, but I will remain focused. Meanwhile, I am living in the present moment. Life is always a box of surprises.

Mother

Truth. Nothing is static. There will be victories and failures. We have to learn from each situation and evolve. The secret is to do good always.

Daughter

Yes, I always follow the divine commandments. This brings me peace amid so many difficulties. In my daily life, I summarize my ethical values in two: Loving God over all things and neighbor as yourself.

Mother

You are a fine example for young people. Today, what we see are carefree, disrespectful, disoriented, and disrespectful young people. You are an exception in an increasingly perverted world.

Daughter

Thank you, mom. I learned from you. I will stay that way all my life. Whatever happens, I will always be honest.

Mother

Good, daughter. We have already worked a lot. Let's go home?

Daughter

Yes. Let's go back home. This is our happiest place, despite being very humble.

Mother

I agree. Our house is the best place to stay.


## Daughter of Faith 2

Kitchen

Daughter

The food was delicious. It was great being with you, Mom.

Mother

Thank you, daughter. I think meals are sacred and strengthen family bonds. I'm feeling great after a day of toil. It seems all stress is over.

Daughter

I feel calm, too, Mom. I get happier and more rested. Strengths and hopes are renewed.

Mother

How nice. Everything is fine with you? Want to tell something?

Daughter

Good thing you took the initiative. You are my mother and my best friend. I know I can vent with you.

Mother

Of course, daughter. I am ready to listen.

Daughter

I already had three boyfriends. Each of them lets me down. The first was a drug addict who didn't work and didn't respect his mother.

Mother

Why did you make that mistake, daughter?

Daughter

You know the men. They are disguised. He made up a story and I ended up believing it. When I first met him, I was already involved. Even so, that was no impediment for me to break up.

Mother

What a luck, daughter. You can't trust that kind of man.

Daughter

I add: No man can be trusted. My second boyfriend was a sportsman. Because of him, I had to attend the stadium games to be able to cheer for him. I really hated all this, but had to please my love. It was months of dedication to unrequited love. I found out he had an affair with a boy on the same team. It was a big disappointment. I was exchanged for a man and had the feeling that I was the worst of women. Worst of all were my friends' comments. They said I was guilty of treason. They based this claim on the fact that I made him very free. Instead of being classified as a victim, I was classified as a defendant for being a woman. How sad.

Mother

It is sorrowful. But this is the face of our male-dominated society. Men have all rights, while we have only duties. This is really revolting. That's why I separated from your father.

Daughter

I understand your pain, mother. Still not satisfied with what I had suffered, I got my third boyfriend. He was a very handsome and rich cowboy. I was enchanted at first sight with him. We spent six months together. Until one day I was late on a date with him and the worst happened. He was so rude to me that I almost fainted. I was cursed with the worst words just because I was late. It was a big trauma for me. I hate rude men. I want a caring and understanding man. Someone who truly loves me. Is there even such a thing anymore? Society is so transformed. Today, we live in a competitive and globalized world. A world in which self-centeredness and technology dominate. A world in which casual sex has become more important than dating. It's so sad to see that love these days is rare. Finding a real love is harder than winning the lottery. I do not know what to do. I wish to send everyone to hell and live my life alone. But I'm not independent yet. I don't have a job yet or have finished my studies. I think when I achieve this first goal, I may have another view of life. But for now, things are at a slow and difficult pace.

Mother

Are you happy, my daughter? What do you lack?

Daughter

Yes, I am happy. I love living with you, working as a farmer and studying. But every day I wake up, hopes are renewed. I want to win in life, mom. I want to be a reputable professional, make a lot of money and have a partner. Furthermore, I want to be completely realized.

Mother

You will have it all, you can be sure. However, things are not as we planned. Only God knows the day of our victory. It takes patience, engagement with projects, honesty, and love in what you do. I believe you. You are an excellent girl. God will prepare good things for you.

Daughter

I have hope, my mother. I pray to God every day that he will bless me on this path.

Mother

He will hear you. Now, I need a favor from you. We are without water. Could you go to the lake and get some water?

Daughter

Of course, yes. I'm leaving immediately. I promise to come as soon as possible.

Mother

Thanks. You are an exemplary daughter.

Field Lake

Adan

Hi, Mary. Where are you going?

Mary

I'm going to get water for my mother.

Adan

That's nice of you. Can I accompany you?

Mary

Of course, you are my friend. It will be an honor.

Lake

Adan

Mary, I've been paying attention to you in the classroom. You look sad and thoughtful. Is something happening?

Mary

These are personal problems. I want to avoid tormenting you with my things.

Adan

Smoothly. You can trust me. I'm your friend. Never forget that. What is happening?

Mary

Are some rudeness that bore me occasionally. Many of them will only disturb those who really study.

Adan

I agree. But don't worry about it. This is normal in a classroom. Focus on your goal and forget about others. You are bigger than them.

Mary

Thank you so much for the advice. I like to be your classmate. You are too kind.

Adan

You can count on me for whatever you want. I admire hardworking people like you. It motivates me a lot. Our region is very needy. It takes a lot of strength and courage to not give up.

Mary

Truth. Keep fighting, too. Studies can transform our trajectory.

Adan

All right, friend. I promise I won't give up.


## Episode 3– Daughter of Faith

Washing clothes in the river

Old woman

I am old and without strength. However, I still do the laundry. What an ungrateful fate, my God!

Mary

Don't fret! Think of all the experience you have accumulated over the years. Think about the positive side of life.

Old woman

Your young people are very optimistic. I admire

your willingness. But that does not work for me. I've been through a lot of suffering, and that's why I no longer believe it.

Mary

I understand. Each has its story. I hope to be happy in my career.

Old woman

I hope so, girl. Look, you are to be congratulated. I heard that you are one of the most dedicated students in the village.

Mary

Yes, I try hard. I want one day graduating and help my family.

Old woman

Very well. Keep the fight. What career do you want to pursue?

Mary

I admire several areas. I admire the work of the cops, doctors, and judges. I think I'll choose one of these areas.

Old woman

I want to avoid discouraging you, but these areas are very difficult for a poor student to study. These are highly competitive areas.

Mary

No problem. I love to face giant challenges. I trust in the God of the impossible. He can do it for me.

Old woman

You are a great woman. I admire you very much.

Mary

Thanks. I need your advice. What precautions should I take to avoid further suffering in life?

Old woman

I don't know if there is a way to avoid suffering. I think what has to happen, happens. But when it comes to success in life, the important thing is to be cautious, have courage, strength, and faith. We can transform anything through our actions.

Mary

I understand. I will follow your advice. I will act instead of waiting. I will plan and have patience. I hope it works.

Old woman

I'm rooting for you. I failed in my dreams, but that doesn't mean the same will happen to you. Each has its story.

Mary

I'm so sorry. But one of the factors that harmed you was staying in that region. Here there is no possibility of success. We are one of the largest pockets of misery in the world.

Old woman

Good analysis. Our region is economically stagnant. Among the main factors of this are drought, corruption, and lack of investment.

Mary

Does one day that change? I wished to see a strong and powerful northeast Brazil. A place developed economically so that their children did not have to emigrate to the southeast of the country.

Old woman

It is not known. It may take a long time for this to happen. Furthermore, it is not the interest of the elites that the northeast be developed. Remember that in society, the poor finance the luxuries of the rich.

Mary

Truth. This is how capitalism works. To change this, a total inversion of values is required. We are not prepared for it. It is more convenient for the rich to stay as is.

Old woman

Truth. It is they who control the state. This increases inequality more and more.

Mary

Good remark. It's time for us to leave. We have finished the work, and we need to study for a test.

Old woman

Truth. Well remembered. I will warn my granddaughter to study with you. She also needs to get good grades.

Mary

It's ok! I'll be waiting for her. It will be an honor to share this good time.

Terrace- studying at home

Classmate

It was a great afternoon of study. I don't know how to thank you for your help. You were very kind.

Daughter

No need to thank. It was also helpful to me. I hope we succeed.

Classmate

This is already right. We are very intelligent.

Daughter

So be it.

Classmate

It's getting close to finish the school year. What do you intend to do after this?

Daughter

I'm not certain. I wish not to stop studying. Furthermore, I want to graduate and help my family. And you?

Classmate

I want to marry. My boyfriend is rich and can support me. But I find your attitude very brave and praiseworthy. An independent woman is always respected.

Daughter

Thanks. How can I continue my studies? I have so many doubts.

Classmate

Go live in a big city. Opportunities are best for you to attend your preferred college. Have no fear. Your family will understand.

Daughter

I think you are right. Although I love my northeastern backcountry, I have no chance here. We have no infrastructure or opportunities. I think this is the only solution.

Classmate

Believe it, friend. Nothing is difficult for those who fight. However, it is necessary to plan well. Try to get a job to cover your expenses. In the big city, everything is costly.

Daughter

Yes. I will think of all the details. I have relatives who live in São Paulo. Maybe they will help me in adapting to this new life.

Classmate

It's always good to have allies. After all, I think it will not be easy. It is an entirely different and dangerous world. I know São Paulo. I spend the last vacation there.

Daughter

I imagine. If I want to win, I have to overcome all the difficulties. I'm going to the end of the world to pursue my dream and whatever happens.

Classmate

That's the spirit, friend. Do you know why I admire you so much? You are an example of dedication and struggle. An honest and valorous girl. His fame spread throughout the region. Stay firm in your dreams and don't worry about the time. He is your ally immediately.

Daughter

I admire you as well. In fact, all the countrymen deserve our consideration. We are a suffering and struggling people. We believe in a better world despite all the difficulties we face. The countryman is a fort.

Classmate

Yes. We are already winners. See you later! Good luck on your test!

Daughter

Good luck to you too.


# Episode 4

Living room

Daughter

Mom, I have some news to give!

Mom

What is it, daughter? So, you make me anxious.

Daughter

I passed all the tests. I now graduated from high school.

Mom

How wonderful! I am proud of you. What are your next plans?

Daughter

It is at this point I'm getting at. I intend to leave for the southeast of the country. I want to get work and attend college of my dreams. Furthermore, I want to be a judge someday to defend the cause of the poor.

Mom

I understand! It is a great pain for a mother to see her daughter go. But you are right. In the situation in which northeast Brazil finds itself, there is no hope of success. I support your decision.

Daughter

Glad to have your support. It was all I needed at this difficult time. I love my northeast. I was born here with great pride and always fought for the good of all. Especially at this time when we are experiencing a major drought. The scenario is terrible even for the most optimistic. Water is lacking, animals are dying and many are leaving in an attempt to survive. We are living in great chaos with no solution. The blame is of poor planning and lack of state incentive. We are totally abandoned and aimless.

Mom

True, daughter. Thank you for your commitment. It's really a shame you have to move. You will be much missed in everyone's life, especially in my life.

Daughter

I know that, mom. I will miss everyone, too. But life demands decisions from us. I hope being right in my choices this time.

Mom

Hopefully, daughter. I wish you all the luck in the world. You are worthy of success.

Daughter

Thank you. I love you so much.

Mom

I love you too, daughter.

Bus station

Woman

You look sorrowful, girl. What is happening?

Mary

It is very difficult to leave all my life story behind. I am definitely moving to São Paulo searching for my dream. This is a bit traumatic.

Woman

This is normal. But if your dream is more important, it will be worth it. Just think about the future. Think of the good things you will know and experience. Each achievement is a new learning. Have such spirit.

Mary

I'll try my best. And you lady? What are you looking for in São Paulo?

Woman

I will find my children again. Ten years ago, we split up, and I never saw them again. They left lacking job opportunities. They wanted to marry, have a family and have their income. Unfortunately, northeast Brazil does not provide us with a means of survival.

Mary

Truth. It will be a wonderful event. I imagine the thrill of reuniting with his family after so long.

Woman

It will be gorgeous. I was very close with my children. Until now, we talk every day by phone. I miss them so bloody much.

Mary

Very cool. It is a really enchanting story.

Woman

Now tell me a little about your story. Where do you come from, what is your profession, and what are you looking for in São Paulo?

Mary

I come from the hope's place. There, I lived with my mother and worked as a farmer. I'm going to São Paulo searching for my biggest dream: Get a job and to attend the college I want. I am a very humble person. My mother taught me early on the value of studies. This is the only alternative of the poor to improving his life.

Woman

I agree. Studying is something that transforms lives. Take the example of my three children. Illiterate, all left the northeast and arriving in São Paulo began to study. Today they are a doctor, engineer, and businessman. Everyone is successful in their fields. See? Nothing is impossible when we fight for what we want. So, my advice is: Fight for your goal. Sooner or later, you become a big winner.

Mary

Thank you for your words of encouragement. It was all I needed immediately. Leaving my beloved state of Pernambuco is really painful. Knowing that

I will have to face a fundamentally different reality in São Paulo, a dangerous and completely unknown place, causes much anxiety and chills. It really is an adventure worthy of any movie.

Woman

As in the movie, life has big challenges. I was also destitute. I married very young with the love of my life. As my parents were against, I had to flee. The beginning of the relationship was very difficult due to lack of money. But do you know what? I did not care. I wanted to be close to the person I loved. With love, we can overcome the challenges. I got a housekeeping job and my husband got a job as a bricklayer. Thank God we had help from some people on this path. They are angels that providence uses to help us. With financial stability, we can finally plan our family. I had three beautiful children and made a point of teaching the values of honesty. But it was still little. They grew up, gained new directions and didn't forget me. Do it that way with your mother too. Be grateful for her effort.

Mary

I love my mother. She will always be the most important person in my life. Despite the distance, I will not forget it. I will always visit her on vacation. Everything she taught me reverberates in my being. We are part of each other. As soon as I grow up on the professional scale and realize my dreams, I will be able to realize her dreams too. That was the promise I made.

Woman

It is a beautiful attitude. Congratulations! You already have my admiration. Now, let's go to the bus. The time has come for the journey to begin.

Mary

Well remembered! May God bless us on this journey.


## Daughter of Faith 5

In the bus

Daughter

Boy, can you tell me if the trip is too long?

Boy

About three days with small punctual stops. On the way, we will visit many locations and see wonderful landscapes. It is certainly a trip that is very worthwhile.

Daughter

So cool. It's my first long trip. I think I'll like it.

Boy

Certainly. Where are you from, and what are you looking for in São Paulo?

Daughter

I come from the hope's place. I am going to São Paulo, searching for my dreams. Furthermore, I want to study and attend college. I want through studies to improve my life and realize my mother's dreams. We are a very humble family from the northeastern back-hands.

Boy

What a beautiful statement. It inspires me. I am also humble. I'm from Pernambuco coast, and I'm going to São Paulo to work. Furthermore, I want to improve my life and maybe even get married. It seems we have similar goals.

Daughter

Truth. That's perfect. It's nice to meet people with mental vibrations similar to ours. This causes a feeling of warmth and tranquility.

Boy

So. Have you had a boyfriend?

Daughter

I had three boyfriends. In each of these relationships, there were positive and negative points, but none of them prospered. I was a little disappointed with love. So, I decided to focus only on the professional field.

Boy

I understand. I also had bad experiences in relationships. But I think we should always be open to the news. We should not judge anyone for other people's attitudes. Absolutely, no one is equal to anyone. Each of us carries a story worth telling. I also believe in happiness. We are all born with a mission. This mission is to be happy anyway.

Daughters

Fine words, but contrast with a cruel reality. Nowadays, lust has taken over the man. People prefer casual sex to commitment. They prefer money to a true feeling. Prefer appearance to values. We are living in a world where having is better than being. It is easier now to betray and lie then, to be honest. The world is almost lost.

Boy

This is all true, but we will not generalize. There are still good men. Without false modesty, I am one of them. I confess that you are a woman who pleases me in every way. We are not together immediately, by chance. I think it was divine providence. It's up to us to give us a chance.

Daughter

I liked you too. But we must go very calmly. Everything is still very recent. I believe love is a construction and this is our starting point. We will always keep in touch. Maybe in the future we build something meaningful.

Boy

I agree with you. I'll give you my contact, so we can get to know each other better. God bless us.

Daughter

He hears you. What I want most is to be happy.

Arrival at Uncle's House

Daughter

I just arrived from the northeast, uncle. I want to say that I am truly grateful for this opportunity.

Uncle

Thank you very much. Not just anyone who opens the doors of your home to strangers. It's a little awkward because I'm separated and people are pretty mean.

Daughter

Strange? Is this how you receive me?

Uncle

It's nothing against you, niece. It is a way of speaking. We have been away for twenty years, and since then, we have not lived. You are taking advantage of my goodwill to prosper. I hope you are grateful.

Daughter

No doubt. You're right. We are just strangers. I promise won't be any trouble. I hope to get a job as soon as possible and have my own home.

Uncle

That day, I'm going to celebrate. My favorite thing is to have my privacy, and I'm giving up that right for you. Always think about it.

Daughter

What should I do? Do you need any help?

Uncle

Very well. I like willing people. Go wash the bathroom and prepare dinner. I want service well done.

Daughter

All right, uncle. I'll do it immediately.

WC

Daughter

Damn old man. I have seen that my days will not be easy. Why do I have to go through this, my God? If I could afford it, I wouldn't humiliate myself so much. I have to be very patient. I think I should look at this as proofs among the many I have been living. As the saying goes, "God writes right on crooked lines." I'm sure the day of my victory will come.

Daughter

I have completed this task. Now, I go to the kitchen to prepare dinner.

Kitchen

I thank my holy mother for teaching me to cook. I am preparing for my uncle a regional recipe. Furthermore, I'm sure he will love it. He doesn't deserve it, but I have to please the host.

Eating

The food was really delicious. I am proud of myself. I will replenish my strength and leave. Furthermore, I need to know a little about the city.

Living room

Daughter

I completed my tasks. Now, I want to meet my boyfriend.

Uncle

It's ok. Come back early. At most ten o'clock at night. I need sleep to work tomorrow.

Daughter

That's right. I promise I'll come soon. A great night!

Uncle

Good night to you, too.

## Daughter of faith 6

Night with boyfriend- restaurant

Mary

Very nice of you to have invited me. It's a great chance to get to know each other better.

Boy

It is a great honor. I had promised to keep in touch. I am a man who keeps his word.

Mary

How nice. That was one of his qualities that caught my attention. This is so rare today.

Boy

Thanks for the compliment. Now tell me. How is your adaptation?

Mary

This is the first day. I feel happy despite all the difficulties. On the way here, I had the opportunity to see incredible landscapes. The city's gigantism impresses and scares me. I'm glad I have your friendship.

Boy

I am flattered by your consideration. We can move forward in this life project and strengthen emotional ties. You caught my eye from the first time I saw you. Her simplicity and innocence make you a unique woman. I will not find any similar woman here in São Paulo. So, I want to invest in that relationship.

Mary

Thankfully, I found you. This is the best time of my life. It is my moment of struggle, searching for my dreams. I sincerely wish someone to be part of this process. Someone who encourages me and who believes in me. Someone to fight my battles against the wickedness of the world. Anyway, be my companion at all hours.

Boy

It will be a great pleasure to be part of this story. In advance, you already have all my admiration. You are brave and dreamy. I need someone with those qualities.

Mary

Thank you. Let's have some fun?

Boy

Good idea. Let's dance to this beautiful song.

Mary

I need to go home. My uncle is waiting.

Boy

It's ok. A good night for you.

Mary

I wish the same for you. The night was delightful. Then we arranged another meeting. Starting tomorrow, I will look for work and enroll in college.

Boy

Very well. Go ahead. I will be rooting for your success.

Mary

Thanks. See you later!

Boy

Until another day.

Travel agency

Clerk

Good morning, darling. What do you want?

Mary

I came register me. I want to get my first job.

Clerk

Could you tell me your name, you're schooling and what area do you want to work?

Mary

My name is Mary. I finished high school. I want to work in any area. Furthermore, I think every job is worthy.

Clerk

Any area? Oh my God! Are you dreaming, girl? People of your color and education only get subordinate services. Put yourself in your place.

Mary

I am a dreamer. I believe in my potential and I know that I can overcome all prejudices. Furthermore, I will still surprise you.

Clerk

Only if you reincarnate several times. The world will remain prejudiced and try to prevent its success. Let's be more rational. I have vacancies as a cleaner, housekeeper, maid, among others. So, let's start with that, shall we?

Mary

It's all right. As I said, I'm not afraid of work. I want to earn some money.

Clerk

Good to hear that. There is an employer with vacancies. Are you willing to do an interview?

Mary

Of course, yes. Just give me the address, dates, and times available.

Clerk

It's all right. Go to Paulista Avenue, building of evidence, apartment 50, Third floor. The meeting will be today, at 2 p.m.

Mary

Thanks for the information and service. I'm already going there.

Office room

Mistress

Do you mean you're the new job applicant?

Mary

I am myself. You can trust me. I'm a great professional. I have a lot of honor. Furthermore, I came from the northeast of the country.

Mistress

How nice. Is this your first job?

Mary

Yes. It is my first formal job. Before, I worked as a farmer.

Mistress

Do you have time availability?

Mary

Yes. I can work full time, six days a week. I want to take a break at night because I want to go to college. On Sunday, I want to meet my boyfriend.

Mistress

Smoothly. You look like a good woman to me. We pay the minimum wage for functions like yours. We demand dedication, attendance, and commitment.

Mary

I'm not experienced enough, but you can expect a high-quality work from me. I need to work to be able attending college.

Mistress

How nice. What college will you attend?

Mary

I'm going to apply to law school.

Mistress

That sounds kind of a joke. A black woman wanting law school. But I like that. You are ambitious and audacious. You have the profile for the job. Furthermore, you're hired.

Mary

My God! How exciting! I do not know how to thank. Immediately, a movie is playing in my mind. The humiliations and difficulties I went through were many. This is just fantastic.

Mistress

Calm down. You haven't won yet. It's just a job as a

maid. However, don't worry. You are quite young and can grow. I see in front of me a woman determined to win. I will encourage you.

Mary

Thank you. When do I start?

Mistress

Tomorrow morning. Come clean and well-dressed. First impression remains.

Mary

It's ok. See you tomorrow.

Mistress

See you later.


## Daughter of faith 7

At work

Husband sung

Boss

What did you do today, girl?

Mary

I did all the housework. I washed, pressed clothes, cooked, took care of the animals, took care of the garden and even kept my mistress company. Furthermore, I think I've done a lot.

Boss

What's your name? Are you sure you have done enough?

Mary

My name is Mary, and I am from the northeast of the country. What do you mean by that?

Boss

You are gorgeous. I also need your services. I feel alone and helpless. My wife only thinks about work and leaves me alone. You don't know what I suffer. Please help me and give me a little affection.

Mary

I have no responsibility to you. My job is to do the housework. Besides, I have a commitment. I'm dating.

Boss

Do you mean you refuse to help me? It's all right. So, I don't have any choice. I will report you for theft.

Mary

What? How dare you offend me that way? I never stole anything from anyone. I am an honest woman.

Boss

I have all the evidence. I put a diamond ring in your bag. I just have to go to the police station and report it.

Mary

Would you be able to do such a thing?

Boss

Foolish girl! I am capable of worse things. But I will give you a chance. I forget that you rejected me if you change your mind. I guarantee that our relationship will be confidential. No one will know. You can continue with your boyfriend. My only interest is sex. I want to own your wonderful body.

Mary

I have no alternative but to accept. If I get arrested or lose my job, my dreams fall apart. I need to keep fighting to be able to change my life. May God forgive you.

Boss

I don't need anyone's forgiveness. Our meetings will be after college, once a week. I'll wait for you near the building, and we'll go to the motel. Believe me: You will like my caresses.

Mary

Monster! I feel dirty with all of this.

Boss

Don't be rebellious! Don't you want to be a great woman? You have to go through life's difficulties. I swear, if you can, I'll applaud you.

Mary

I will try very hard for you to applaud. I'm confident that I will overcome all of this. You will be just a stain on my past that no one will ever know.

Boss

Or I will be a good memory. Never know. Occasionally, what looks bad can become good.

Mary

That's what we'll see. I'm going to school. I already finished my work.

Boss

Go in peace. I'll meet you at the exit. Today is our first date. Don't tell anyone, or you are a dead woman.

Mary

Keep calm. No one will know.

School

Clerk

Good evening. What do you want, miss?

Mary

I would like to study law. How is the selection process?

Clerk

The student makes a registration and takes an admission test. I must remember that we are a private school. Are you sure what you said? The monthly fees are quite high.

Mary

What is the cost?

Clerk

The monthly fee is two minimum wages. What do you say?

Mary

I cannot afford. I would need an eighty percent discount to be able to attend.

Clerk

Why would we do that?

Mary

I ask you to have mercy. I am desperate. Furthermore, I am a northeastern girl who came to São Paulo fleeing the drought and searching for my dreams. I need a chance. I need someone to bet on me. Furthermore, I need someone who has humanity and helps me. I don't have another chance beyond that.

Clerk

I am the director of the course. We can only make an exception if you are an exceptional student. I will make available three scholarships discounted of eighty percent for the best grades. I'm entering you for proof. Furthermore, I want to see what you're capable of.

Mary

I am grateful for this chance. I promise you won't regret it. When the test will be?

Clerk

In a month. Good luck to you.

Mary

Thank you. I'll need.

One month later

school

The race day has arrived. I hope I have good luck.

Living room

Boyfriend

What's up? How was the proof?

Mary

There were forty questions on high school subjects. I felt very comfortable, confident, and peaceful. I think I did well.

Boyfriend

How nice. When is the result going out?

Mary

Twenty days from now. Until then, I will have to control my great anxiety. What scared me was the great competition. There were more than five thousand candidates running for scholarship.

Boyfriend

My God! There were many competitors. But do not worry. You are already a big winner.

Mary

Yes, I feel victorious. Now, I will continue with my routine. Then I'll let you know the result.

Boyfriend

I'll be rooting for you, love. All luck to you.

Mary

Thank you. I love you.

Boyfriend

Love you too.


## Daughter of faith 8

With the boyfriend

Mary

Love, I just heard some wonderful news. I won the scholarship. I was able to take the first step in the pursuit of my dreams. Furthermore, I'm going to law school!

Nam

Congratulations! I always knew your ability. I will be together with you, love.

Mary

Thank you. Your company is critical to me. With you, I feel complete.

Flirt

I love you too. The more time passes, we discover more things in common. It was a blessing to have met you.

Mary

It's been an incredible experience. Hopefully, our relationship will bear fruit. It really changed my life.

Nam

My life has also been transformed. Let's move on together.

First day of school

Teacher

Welcome to law school. My name is Catherine. I am the teacher of constitutional law. I would like to say that I am pleased with the presence of you all. If you're here, it is because already are winners.

Mary

Thank you, teacher. You don't know what a thrill I am feeling here. I was a farmer and came from the northeast of the country searching for my dream. Arriving here, I found a world fundamentally different from what I imagined. I had to adapt, I got a job, and I'm starting college. Each achievement is critical to me. Although my trajectory be only at the beginning, I already feel like a winner.

Teacher

You are proof that our teaching is being democratized. Previously, blacks and women were not part of the academic world. This is a perverse inheritance of a completely elitist society. This refers to all areas.

Mary

It's about time. I hope to remain fighting for my dreams.

Student

I find this totally clueless. For me, colored place is in the kitchen. This stigma cannot be changed in such a short time.

Teacher

This is prejudice on your part. We can change this story, even if gradually. The important thing is to make our colleague at ease. She needs to believe in her dreams. This is very commendable.

Student

You're right. Forgive me, Mary, you have all our support.

Mary

Thank you. I'll do my best. You will be part of a beautiful story.

Teacher

So be it. Now, let's start the class.

Expulsion from home

Uncle

Where were you, girl? You kept me waiting all night.

Mary

Forgive me, uncle. I lost time talking to my boyfriend. I promise that this will not be repeated.

Uncle

Of course, it won't be repeated. You can pack up and go. I just can't stand the sight of him anymore.

Mary

My God! What will become of me? I have nowhere to go.

Uncle

Go to your boyfriend's house, or anywhere you want. Here you have no more space. There's no more a piece of cake.

Mary

It's ok. Thank you for your hospitality. I have no regrets.

Uncle

I'm glad. Good luck with your projects. I'll be rooting for you.

Mary

Thank you! Be at peace, uncle!

Boyfriend's house

Mary

I was kicked out of the house. Can you help me?

Nam

Of course, my love. Feel free. I just didn't expect it would be so soon.

Mary

Yeah. These are surprises that life provides us. Shall we try to live as husband and wife?

Nam

I'm in! There must be some reason why life has brought us together. We will try to live this union. I'm sure we're on the right track.

Mary

We will try! God bless us.

Meeting with the boss

Mary

I wanted to say that it was all over. I want to avoid being your lover anymore.

Pat

Why? We were getting along so well.

Mary

I'm living with another man and I need to respect him. I will be faithful at all costs.

Pat

You already know the result. You are fired. Furthermore, you can look for another job.

Mary

Smoothly. What I can't do is stay that way. That won't bring me down.

Pat

Good luck to you. You are welcome to see yourselves out.

Boyfriend's house

Mary

I just lost my job. I think I'm going to have to leave college.

Nam

No way. As long as you don't get a new job, I will help you. That's what spouses are for. To support each other in difficult times.

Mary

I'm truly thankful. I promise I won't settle. Furthermore, I will speak to the course director. Maybe he does give me any support.

Nam

Good idea. Even if you can't, don't give up. There are many jobs in São Paulo. One of these opportunities can be yours. We will fight together.

Mary

Thank you. I don't know what would become of me without your support. You are a spectacular man.

Nam

You that are wonderful. I am pleased to live with you. Gradually, we grow together. The union is who makes the strength.

Mary

My dear gift from God, I will reward you when you're a great woman. I will make all your dreams come true.

Nam

Amen. May God hear you.


## Daughter of faith 9

Meeting with the director
Director

Very well. May I know the reason for this meeting?

Mary

I want to ask for some support. I am out of work and need guidance.

Director

What is your work experience?

Mary

I worked as a farmer and domestic. But I'm attending law school. I believe I can work on anything.

Director

Very interesting. You look like a hard-working young woman. I think I have a job in the college secretary. Do you want the job?

Mary

I'd love to. I need money to pay for college. Furthermore, I do not know how to thank you.

Director

No need to thank. Just work hard. We pay only a minimum wage. So, I think that will help in some way.

Mary

It is a great help. I promise not to disappoint.

Director

My advice is to keep studying. Make public tenders. The salary is much better.

Mary

I wrote it down mentally and I will follow your advice. I need to win anyway. Furthermore, I need to overcome poverty with my efforts. I deserve.

Director

Good luck with your projects. I will work now. Until another day.

Mary

See you later!

I work in the secretariat

Mary

Good morning. I came to exercise my position. What's your name?

Helena

My name is Helena, and I am head of the office. I didn't know we had a new employee. Who hired you?

Mary

The college directness.

Helena

My God! What was she thinking? This Department is a reputable institution. I don't see you with the job requirements.

Mary

Why that? Why am I black? What is the problem?

Helena

It is not a chase. But we need to maintain traditions. Blacks are not welcome here.

Mary

I got the message. I'm leaving immediately. But the world takes many turns. I'll get over this.

Helena

I wish the best for you. Go in peace!

Meeting with her boyfriend

Mary

My love, I am desolate. I don't work at any job. Everyone rejects me.

Nam

Let's just calm down for a second. It is not yet the end of the world. You will get over it.

Mary

What is your suggestion?

Nam

You've had a good education. Try public tenders.

Mary

You are the second person who tells me this. I think I will dedicate myself more. It is certainly the best alternative.

Nam

Yeah. As a good husband, I will support you in your decisions.

Mary

Thank you. You are my piece of heaven. I don't know what I would do without you.

Nam

I love you too. Let's move on with our projects.

Library

storyteller

Mary started studying for public tenders. In front of it, there was the opportunity for financial improvement. The public tender was democratic. The one with the most capacity would exercise public office.

With plenty of time, he began to devote herself completely to this project. His good school background helped him a lot. With that, she was consumed the didactic contents. With a year of preparation, she had already participated in ten public tenders. It was approved in all competitions. Now, she was expecting to be summoned to begin work.

With the husband

Mary

My love, I have just been summoned to the position of my dreams. I'm going to be a bailiff.

Nam

How wonderful! Congratulations! Didn't I say it was worth it?

Mary

You were absolutely right. I am now an independent woman. I will earn five minimum wages.

Nam

It's a great start. But don't get too comfortable. You can grow even more.

Mary

Truth. My dream is to be a judge. I want to apply the right in favor of minorities. I feel it is my mission.

Nam

So, move on. Congratulations one more time.

Mary

I will start working. I need money.

Nam

Go with God.

Taking over

Mentor

With this authorization, you can be now to take office. Congratulations.

Mary

This is a milestone in my life. I am leaving misery and starting a new phase. Right now, it's like a movie is playing in my mind. It is so gratifying to know that this achievement is the result of my efforts.

Mentor

I wonder how difficult it must have been. Congratulations on your achievement. You can be an example for all black women in our country. You have to believe in your dreams.

Mary

Yes. I will continue to believe in my dreams. I will go even further. You can believe that.

Mentor

I don't doubt. Much peace, success, health and happiness in your life!

Mary

Thank you. You are too kind.

At work

Mary

Good morning, I'm the new employee of the office. All right?

Boss

All right. Be welcome. I'm the head of the sector. Whatever you need me, I'm at your disposal.

Mary

Thanks.

Boss

What are your qualifications?

Mary

I am studying in law school.

Boss

Very well. You chose the right course. With work experience, you will be able to grow even more. We have a very good and competent team. We will accompany you in your adaptation process.

Mary

I am grateful for that. Here begins a new story.


## Daughter of faith episode 10

Inauguration Ceremony

Master of ceremony

Today, you become a judge. Got something to say?

Mary

Today, is a day of joy. It is the day of my inauguration as a judge. It is the achievement of a goal pursued for years. I can't exactly say how I feel. I just know it feels really good. I got overcome the barriers of poverty and prejudice. I became one of the few successful black women. I am proud of my effort and hope that this will serve as an example for the entire Brazilian community. Keep on pursuing your goals. If I succeeded, you can achieve it too. Just fight and believe.

Master of ceremony

Congratulations! You are worthy. As a student in law school, you showed what you were capable of. I am proud to have followed your winning trajectory and tell you to continue specializing. You are a limitless being. Could you speak your first profession to the public?

Mary

I was a farmer. I also worked in other manual professions. I am very proud of my history and where I came from. I am a northeastern warrior who overcame difficulties.

Master

What is the secret to success?

Mary

My willpower and my husband's support. For sure, it was my best achievement.

Husband

Thank you very much, woman. You are also a great companion. Since I met you, my world is colorful. I don't exchange you for money or any other good.

Mary

I love you too. I am very excited about all of this. God heard my prayers.

Husband

You are worthy. You are a very warrior woman.

Master

The good girls always win. Follow her example, my people. We need to follow valiant women like this.

Mary

Thank you very much to all. Now, I have to fulfill a mission.

Northeast

mother

My daughter, how long I haven't seen you. What good news brings you here?

Mary

I came to tell you that I'm working as a judge. I also came to introduce you to my husband.

Husband

It is a great honor to be here with you. The Northeast is really a charming place.

Mother

I'm happy for you, daughter. Didn't I say you could do it? I'm very proud of you.

Daughter

Thank you, my mother. Do you want to live with us? It would be an honor.

Mother

don't want to, daughter. I like it is from the northeast. I am a sprout of this land that the world has forgotten. The northeast is full of cultures, legends and life. We have frevo, maracatu, baião, carnival, June parties and literary tradition. We are the heart of Brazilian culture.

Daughter

I love my northeast too. I understand your decision. But I will keep my promise. I will make your dreams come true.

Mother

Thank you, daughter of faith. May God enlighten you on your way.

Daughter

I just wanted a fairer world. A world in which people are not judged by their race, sexual orientation, religion, gender or any other particularity. We are all the same.

Husband

It's a little utopian, love. The world will always be uneven. But you can make a difference through your actions.

Daughter

You're right. I promise I'll try my best. I will judge fairly, allowing many people to have their requests fulfilled. I will contribute to a better world.

Mother

Cheers, daughter. Your story is inspiring.

Mary

This is a milestone in my life. I am leaving misery and starting a new phase. Immediately, it's like a movie is playing in my mind. It is so gratifying to know that this achievement is the result of my efforts.

Mentor

I wonder how difficult it must have been. Congratulations on your achievement. You can be an example for all black women in our country. You have to believe in your dreams.

Mary

Yes. I will continue to believe in my dreams. I will go even further. You can believe that.

Mentor

I don't doubt. Much peace, success, health, and happiness in your life!

Mary

Thank you. You are too kind.

At work

Mary

Good morning, I'm the new employee of the office. All right?

Boss

All right. Be welcome. I'm the head of the sector. Whatever you need me, I'm at your disposal.

Mary

Thanks.

Boss

What are your qualifications?

Mary

I am studying in law school.

Boss

Very well. You chose the right course. With work experience, you will be able to grow even more. We have an excellent and competent team. We will accompany you in your adaptation process.

Mary

I am grateful for that. Here begins a new story.

Daughter of Faith episode 10

Inauguration Ceremony

Master of ceremony

Today, you become a judge. Do you have something to say?

Mary

Today, is a day of joy. It is the day of my inauguration as a judge. It is the achievement of a goal pursued for years. I can't exactly say how I feel. I just know it feels perfect. Furthermore, I got overcome the barriers of poverty and prejudice. I became one of the few successful black women. I am proud of my effort and hope that this will serve as an example for the entire Brazilian community. Keep on pursuing your goals. If I succeeded, you can achieve it too. Just fight and believe.

Master of ceremony

Congratulations! You are worthy. As a student in law school, you showed what you were capable of. I am proud to have followed your winning trajectory and tell you to continue specializing. You are a limitless being. Could you speak your first profession to the public?

Mary

I was a farmer. I also worked in other manual professions. Furthermore, I am very proud of my history and where I came from. I am a northeastern warrior who overcame difficulties.

Master

What is the secret to success?

Mary

My willpower and my husband's support. For sure, it was my best achievement.

Husband

Thank you very much, woman. You are also a great companion. Since I met you, my world is colorful. I don't exchange you for money or any other good.

Mary

I love you too. Furthermore, I am very excited about all of this. God heard my prayers.

Husband

You are worthy. You are a very warrior woman.

Master

The good girls always win. Follow her example, my people. We need to follow valiant women like this.

Mary

Thank you very much to all. Now, I have to fulfill a mission.

Northeast

mother

My daughter, how long I haven't seen you. What good news brings you here?

Mary

I came to tell you that I'm working as a judge. I also came to introduce you to my husband.

Husband

It is a great honor to be here with you. The Northeast is really a charming place.

Mother

I'm happy for you, daughter. Didn't I say you could do it? I'm very proud of you.

Daughter

Thank you, my mother. Do you want to live with us? It would be an honor.

Mother

Don't want to, daughter. I like it is from the northeast. I am a sprout of this land that the world has forgotten. The northeast is full of cultures, legends, and life. We have frevo, maracatu, baião, carnival, June parties and literary tradition. We are the heart of Brazilian culture.

Daughter

I love my northeast, too. I understand your decision. But I will keep my promise. I will make your dreams come true.

Mother

Thank you, daughter of faith. May God enlighten you on your way.

Daughter

I just wanted a fairer world. A world in which people are not judged by their race, sexual orientation, religion, gender or any other particularity. We are all the same.

Husband

It's a little utopian, love. The world will always be uneven. But you can make a difference through your actions.

Daughter

You're right. I promise I'll try my best. I will judge fairly, allowing many people to have their requests fulfilled. Furthermore, I will contribute to a better world.

Mother

Cheers, daughter. Your story is inspiring.

The end

CPSIA information can be obtained
at www.ICGtesting.com
Printed in the USA
BVHW040902130821
614372BV00014B/287

9 786599 556371